AMERICA'S CHAMPION SWIMMER

· ·

Gertrude Ederle

WRITTEN BY

David A. Adler

ILLUSTRATED BY

Terry Widener

Gulliver Books

Harcourt, Inc.

SAN DIEGO   NEW YORK   LONDON

Library of Congress Cataloging-in-Publication Data
Adler, David A.
America's champion swimmer: Gertrude Ederle/David A. Adler;
illustrated by Terry Widener.
p.   cm.
"Gulliver Books."
Summary: Describes the life and accomplishments of Gertrude Ederle,
the first woman to swim the English Channel and a figure in the early
women's rights movement.
1. Ederle, Gertrude, 1906–   —Juvenile literature.   2. Swimmers—
United States—Biography—Juvenile literature.   3. Women swimmers—
United States—Biography—Juvenile literature.   [1. Ederle, Gertrude,
1906–   . 2. Swimmers.   3. Women—Biography.]
I. Widener, Terry, ill.   II. Title.
GV838.E34A35   2000
797.2'1' 092—dc21
[B]   98-54954
ISBN 0-7398-2197-0 library binding

First edition

F E D C B A

The illustrations in this book were done in Golden acrylics on
Strathmore Bristol board.
The display type was set in Bernhard Gothic and Stuyvesant.
The text type was set in Fournier.
Color separations by Bright Arts Ltd., Hong Kong
Printed and bound by Phoenix Color Corp., Rockaway, New Jersey
This book was printed on totally chlorine-free Nymolla Matte Art paper.
Production supervision by Stanley Redfern
Designed by Michael Farmer

For Mom, a real champion

——D. A. A.

For Kate, Kellee, and girls everywhere—
dream big and believe in yourself

——T. W.

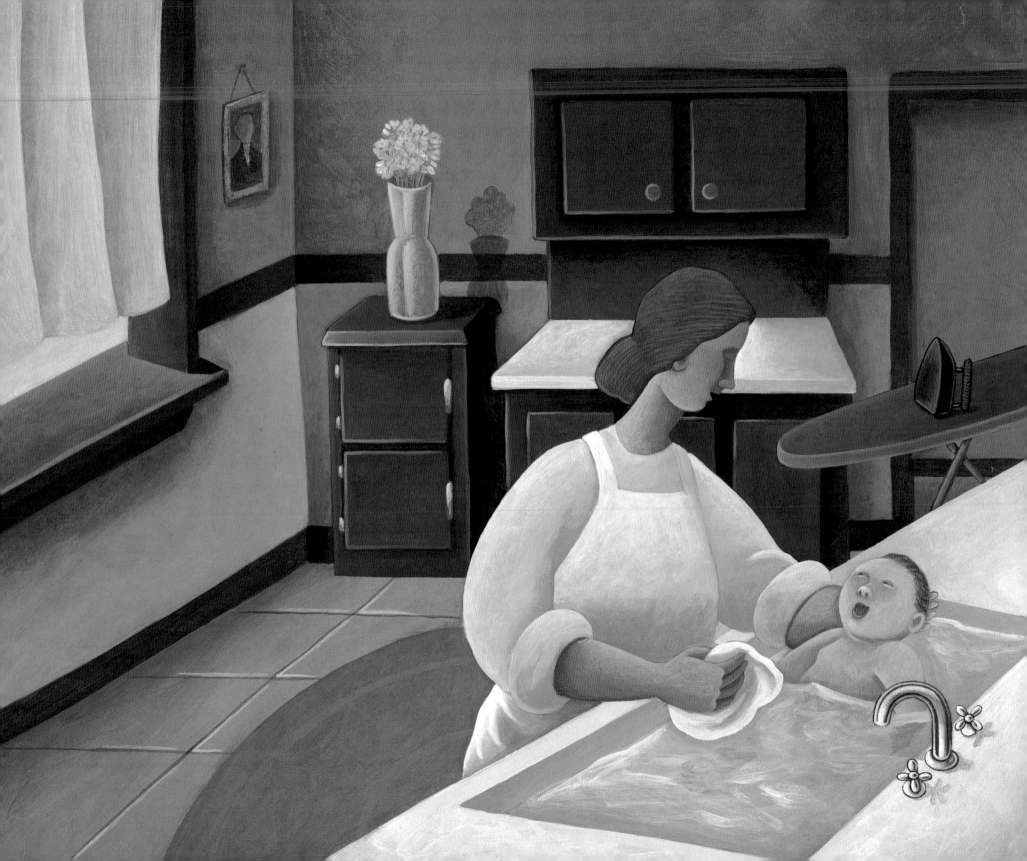

In 1906 women were kept out of many clubs and restaurants. In most states they were not allowed to vote. Many people felt a woman's place was in the home.

But Gertrude Ederle's place was in the water.

Gertrude Ederle was born on October 23, 1906. She was the third of six children and was raised in New York City, where she lived in an apartment next to her father's butcher shop. Her family called her Gertie. Most everyone else called her Trudy.

Trudy spent her early years playing on the sidewalks of New York. It wasn't until she was seven that she had her first adventure in the water. While visiting her grandmother in Germany, Trudy fell into a pond and nearly drowned.

After that near disaster, Trudy's father was determined to teach her to swim. For her first lesson, he tied one end of a rope to Trudy's waist and held on to the other end. He put Trudy into a river and told her to paddle like a dog.

Trudy mastered the dog paddle. She joined her older sister Margaret and the other children in the water and copied their strokes. Soon Trudy swam better than any of them.

From that summer on, it was hard to keep Trudy out of the water. She *loved* to swim. At the age of thirteen she became a member of the New York Women's Swimming Association and took lessons there.

At fifteen Trudy won her first big race.

The next year, she attempted to be the first woman to swim the more than seventeen miles from lower Manhattan to Sandy Hook, New Jersey. When Trudy slowed down, her sister Margaret yelled, "Get going, lazybones!" And Trudy did. She finished in just over seven hours. And she beat the men's record.

People were beginning to notice Gertrude Ederle. Newspapers described her as courageous, determined, modest, and poised. They called her the most perfect swimmer. Trudy's mother said she was "just a plain home girl."

In 1924 this "plain home girl" was good enough to make the U.S. Olympic team. Trudy won three medals at the games in Paris. Her team won more points than all the other countries' swimming teams combined.

By 1925 Trudy had set twenty-nine U.S. and world records. She was determined to take on the ultimate challenge: the English Channel. Many had tried to swim the more-than-twenty-mile-wide body of cold, rough water that separates England from France. But only five men—and no women—had ever made it all the way across.

Many people were sure Trudy couldn't do it. A newspaper editorial declared that Trudy wouldn't make it and that women must admit they would "remain forever the weaker sex."

It didn't matter to Trudy what people said or wrote. She was going to swim the Channel.

Early in the morning on August 18, 1925, Trudy stepped into the water at Cape Gris-Nez, France, the starting point for the swim. For almost nine hours she fought the strong current. Then, when Trudy had less than seven miles to go, her trainer thought she had swallowed too much water and pulled her, crying, from the sea.

Trudy did not give up her dream. She found a new trainer, and a year later, on Friday, August 6, 1926, she was ready to try again.

Trudy wore a red bathing cap and a two-piece bathing suit and goggles that she and her sister Margaret had designed. To protect her from the icy cold water, Margaret coated Trudy with lanolin and heavy grease. The greasing took a long time—too long for Trudy. "For heaven's sake," she complained. "Let's get started."

Finally, at a little past seven in the morning, she stepped into the water. "Gee, but it's cold," Trudy said.

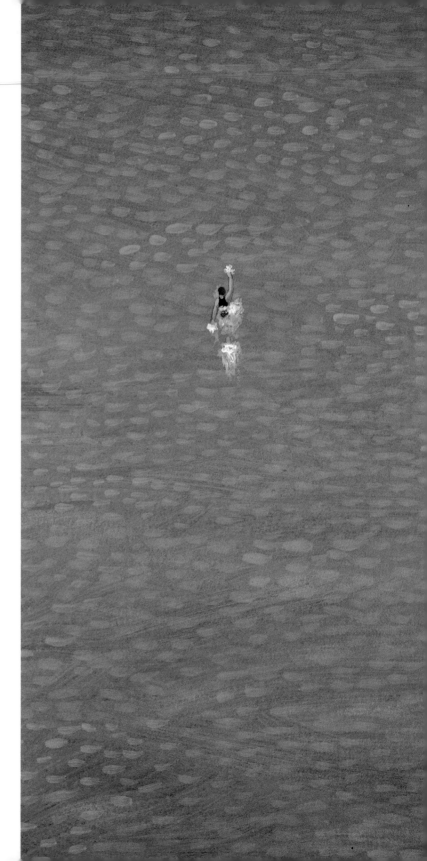

Trudy's father, her sister Margaret, her trainer, and a few other swimmers were on board a tugboat named *Alsace*. The boat would accompany Trudy to make sure she didn't get lost in the fog and was safe from jellyfish, sharks, and the Channel's powerful currents. There was a second boat, too, with reporters and photographers on board.

As the *Alsace* bobbed up and down in the choppy water, Margaret wrote in chalk on the side of the boat, "This way, Ole Kid." She drew an arrow that pointed to England.

OLE KID

To entertain Trudy, Margaret and some of the others sang American songs, including "The Star-Spangled Banner" and "East Side, West Side." Trudy said the songs kept her "brain and spirit good."

At first the sea was calm.

Trudy swam so fast that her trainer was afraid she would tire herself out. He ordered her to slow down.

Trudy refused.

At about ten-thirty in the morning, Trudy had her first meal. She floated on her back and ate chicken and drank beef broth. A while later, she ate chocolate and chewed on sugar cubes. Then she swam on.

At about one-thirty in the afternoon, it started to rain. A strong wind stirred the water. For a while, Trudy would swim forward a few feet only to be pulled back twice as far.

By six o'clock the tide was stronger. The waves were twenty feet high. The rough water made the people aboard the *Alsace* and the news boat seasick.

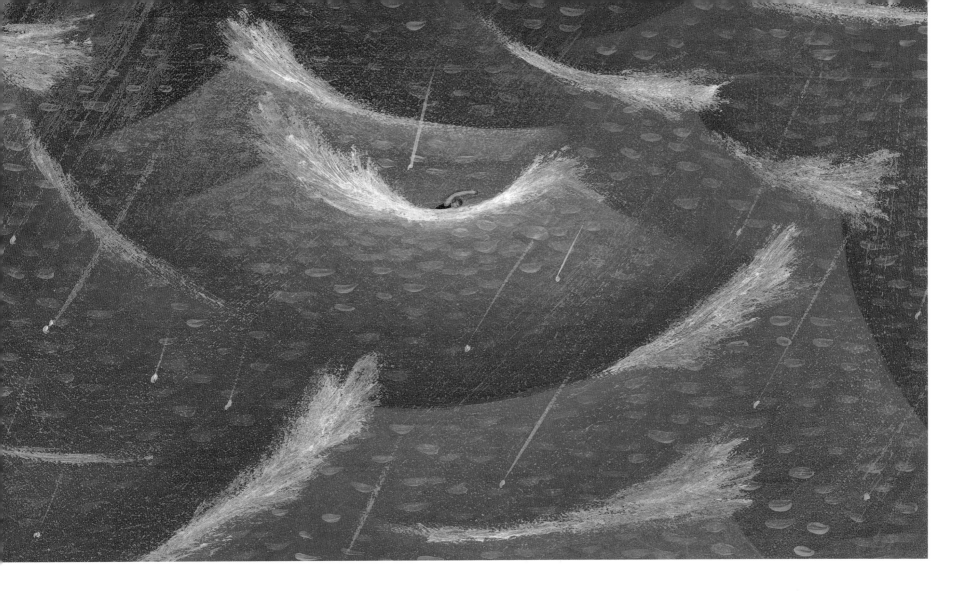

Trudy's trainer was sure she couldn't finish the swim. He told her to give up.

"No, no," Trudy yelled over the sound of the waves. She kept swimming.

In the next few hours, the rain and wind became stronger and the sea rougher. At times the rough water pulled the boats away, out of Trudy's sight. She was scared. It was eerie being out there all alone.

Now Trudy began to have trouble kicking in the water. When the *Alsace* came close again, Trudy said her left leg had become stiff. Her trainer was frightened for her. He yelled, "You must come out."

"What for?" Trudy shouted, and kept swimming.

Trudy continued to fight the tide and the constant stinging spray of water in her face. She knew she would either swim the Channel or drown.

As Trudy neared Kingsdown, on the coast of England, she saw thousands of people gathered to greet her. They lit flares to guide her to shore.

At about nine-forty at night, after more than fourteen hours in the water, Trudy's feet touched land. Hundreds of people, fully dressed, waded into the water to greet her. When she reached the shore, her father hugged Trudy and wrapped her in a warm robe.

"I knew if it could be done, it had to be done, and I did it," Trudy said after she got ashore. "All the women of the world will celebrate."

Trudy swam the Channel in just fourteen hours and thirty-one minutes. She beat the men's record by almost two hours. In newspapers across the world, Trudy's swim was called history making. Reporters declared that the myth that women are the weaker sex was "shattered and shattered forever."

Trudy sailed home aboard the SS *Berengaria*. After six days at sea, the ship entered New York Harbor.

Two airplanes circled and tipped their wings to greet Trudy. People on boats of all kinds rang their bells and tooted their horns to salute her. Foghorns sounded.

Trudy climbed into an open car for a parade up lower Broadway. An estimated two million people, many of them women, stood and cheered. They threw scraps of newspaper, ticker tape, pages torn from telephone books, and rolls of toilet paper.

When her car arrived at the New York city hall, Mayor Jimmy Walker

praised Trudy for her courage, grace, and athletic prowess. "American women," he said, "have ever added to the glory of our nation."

President Calvin Coolidge sent a message that was read at the ceremony. He called Trudy "America's Best Girl." And she was. Gertrude Ederle had become a beacon of strength to girls and women everywhere.

Notes from the author:

While it's twenty-one miles across the Channel, the rough water makes the actual swim much longer. It was estimated Trudy had to swim thirty-five miles to get across.

Trudy's 1925 swim was cut short because of terrible conditions and because her trainer, Jabez Wolffe, touched her in the water. That touch disqualified the swim. Wolffe had tried to swim the Channel more than twenty times but had never succeeded.

For the 1926 swim Trudy's trainer was Thomas W. Burgess, who in 1911, after many failed attempts, was the second man to swim the Channel.

Someone who witnessed Trudy's swim and more than a dozen other attempts commented that in good weather Trudy would have finished at least four hours sooner.

A *London Daily News* editorial declared women "the weaker sex" the very day of Trudy's successful 1926 swim. The next day, the newspaper didn't back down from that statement but explained that "Miss Ederle is evidently a superwoman."

According to New York City Police Inspector Kuehne, many women felt empowered by Trudy's swim. At Trudy's welcome back to New York, he tried to help one very old woman. He was afraid she would get hurt in the crowd. "I guess I can take care of myself," she told him. Inspector Kuehne said later, "That seemed to be the attitude of most of the women."

On August 28, 1926, three weeks after Trudy's swim, another woman, Mrs. Millie Corson, left the coast of France. Two other swimmers, both men, made the attempt with her. Only Millie Corson made it across. Millie Corson was the first mother to swim the Channel. She got across in fifteen hours and thirty-two minutes, not fast enough to beat Trudy's record but faster than any of the previous male swimmers. Two days later, on August 30, 1926, Ernst Vierkoetter, a German, swam the Channel. He did it in just twelve hours and forty-three minutes, setting a new record.

Gertrude Ederle never married. She lost much of her hearing after her swim, perhaps because of the cold Channel water but more likely the result of childhood measles. She fell sometime in the 1940s and was in a cast for more than four years. Doctors were sure Trudy would be confined to a wheelchair, but she was determined to walk again—and she did. Trudy worked as a dress designer and taught deaf children to swim. She was also a member of the President's Council on Youth Fitness.

The sources for much of the information for this book were periodicals of the time, including the *New York Times*, the *New York World*, and the *Literary Digest*, as well as more recent collective biographies.

AUSTRALIAN SEA LIFE

FOR MIRO – M. C.

AUSTRALIAN SEA LIFE

Artwork by
MATT CHUN

LITTLE HARE
www.littleharebooks.com

GREAT WHITE SHARK

Great white sharks are the largest predatory fish in the world. They have a fearsome reputation, but are clever, curious animals. In Australia, they are most often found around the lower part of the country, from Southern Queensland to the middle of the Western Australian coastline.

Great white sharks have thick, tough skin that is grey in most places and white on their bellies. Unlike many other sharks, great whites are warm blooded. Their sleek bodies angle towards a pointed snout, and their large, curved dorsal fin slices out of the water when they swim close to the surface.

Their jaws are packed with hundreds of teeth, which grow in multiple rows. Great white sharks consume a wide range of prey, including fish, squid, stingrays, seals, sea lions and dolphins. Their senses are very acute, and they can smell blood in the water across long distances. They use electroreception to hunt – the pores on their snouts are filled with a special kind of jelly that can sense the tiny electrical currents caused by other marine animals moving in the water.

Great white sharks use their gills to breathe – pulling water in through their mouths as they swim, absorbing the oxygen, then passing the water out through their gills. If they stop swimming, their access to fresh, oxygen-filled water also stops, so they need to move constantly.

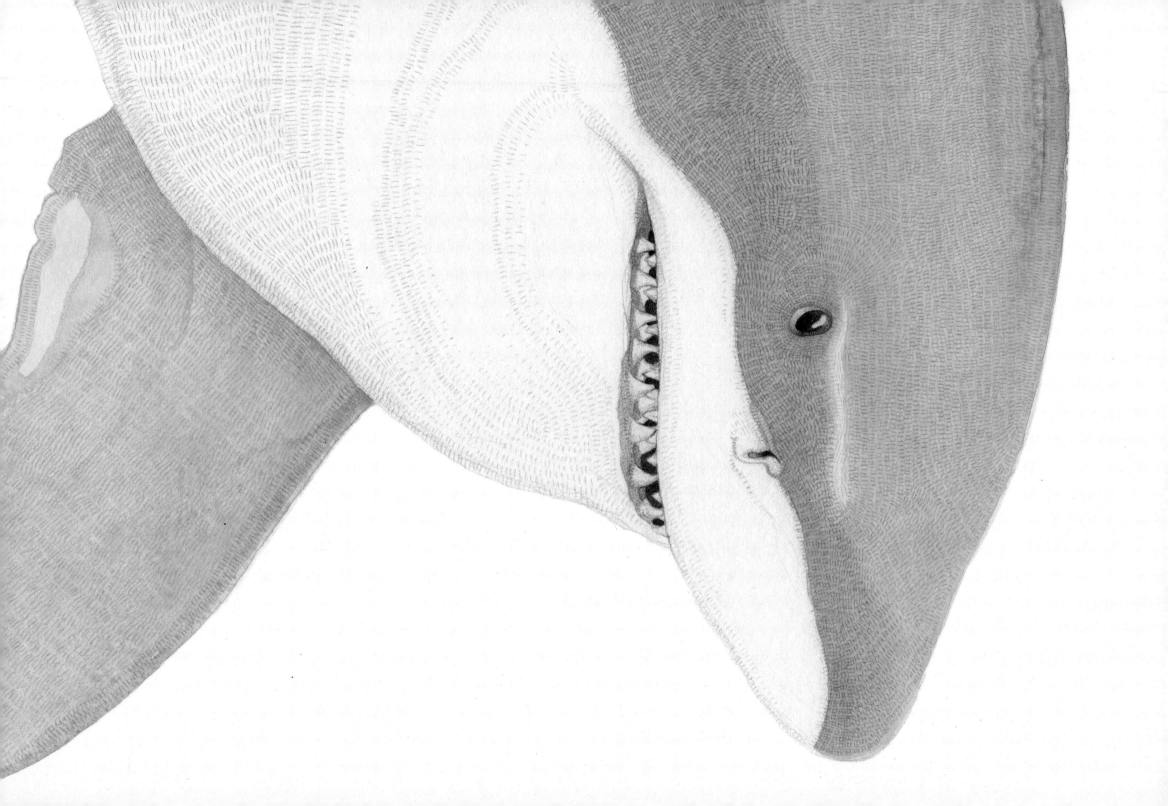

COPPERBAND BUTTERFLY FISH

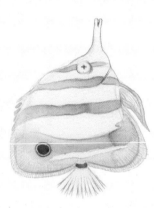

Copperband butterfly fish live in warm, tropical waters, and are often found on coral reefs and rocky shorelines. In Australia, they live along the coast of Queensland and down into the central New South Wales coast. They are particularly common in the Great Barrier Reef.

Large fins at the top and bottom of their bodies give copperband butterfly fish a broad, squared-off appearance at the back – from the front, they are very slender. They have stripes along their bodies in warm shades of orange or yellow, and a dark spot on their dorsal fin called an 'ocellus'. This spot looks a little like an eye; it is often darker in the centre, with a pale blue ring around the outside. This false eye can confuse predators, as it is harder to tell which is the front end of the fish.

Copperband butterfly fish have particularly long, thin snouts, and are sometimes called beaked coralfish. Their snouts are useful for seeking out food in reefs and rocky areas, as they can poke into small spaces. These fish eat very small creatures, including worms, coral polyps and small invertebrates.

Although they are often quite solitary, copperband butterfly fish do form pairs – particularly during breeding season. Eggs are released into the water, where they float along until they hatch. Young fish don't have the characteristic long snout of their species right away – it gets longer as they get older.

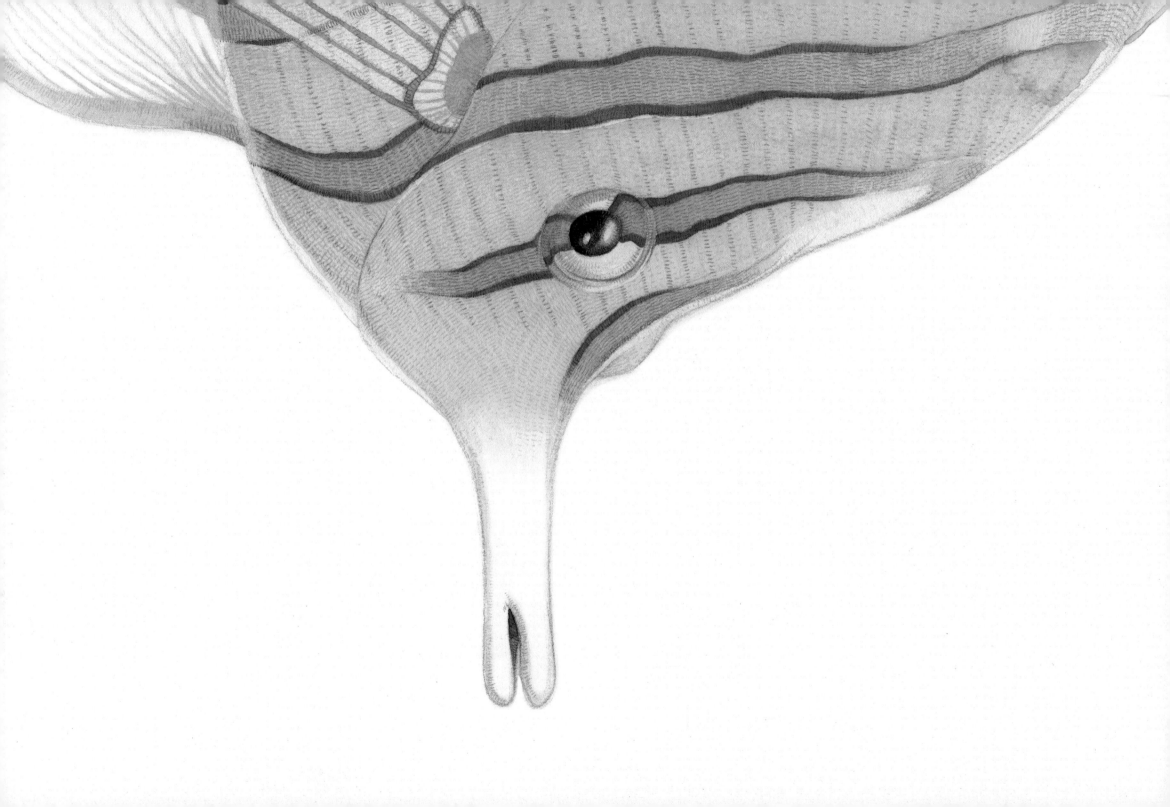

FANFIN ANGLERFISH

The fanfin anglerfish, also called fanfin seadevils or hairy anglerfish, can be found off the coast of New South Wales – in the cold, dark depths. They have rounded bodies in shades of black and brown, and enormous mouths. Their bottom jaws protrude out, and their mouths are packed with thin, incredibly pointy teeth.

The females are much larger than males, and have a glowing lure dangling in front of their faces. They also have long, slender filaments sprouting from their fins that trail out around their bodies, each one with its own nerves and muscles that allow it to move independently.

When they're young, male fanfin anglers find a female and bite firmly into her body. They stay there until their skin fuses together, becoming completely reliant on their female hosts for nutrition – the two fish will eventually even share the same bloodstream.

Food can be difficult to find in the depths of the ocean. Glowing lures help female fanfin anglers prey on things like fish and crustaceans. Their wide jaws allow them to eat creatures of many sizes, and their stomachs are able to stretch to accommodate larger meals.

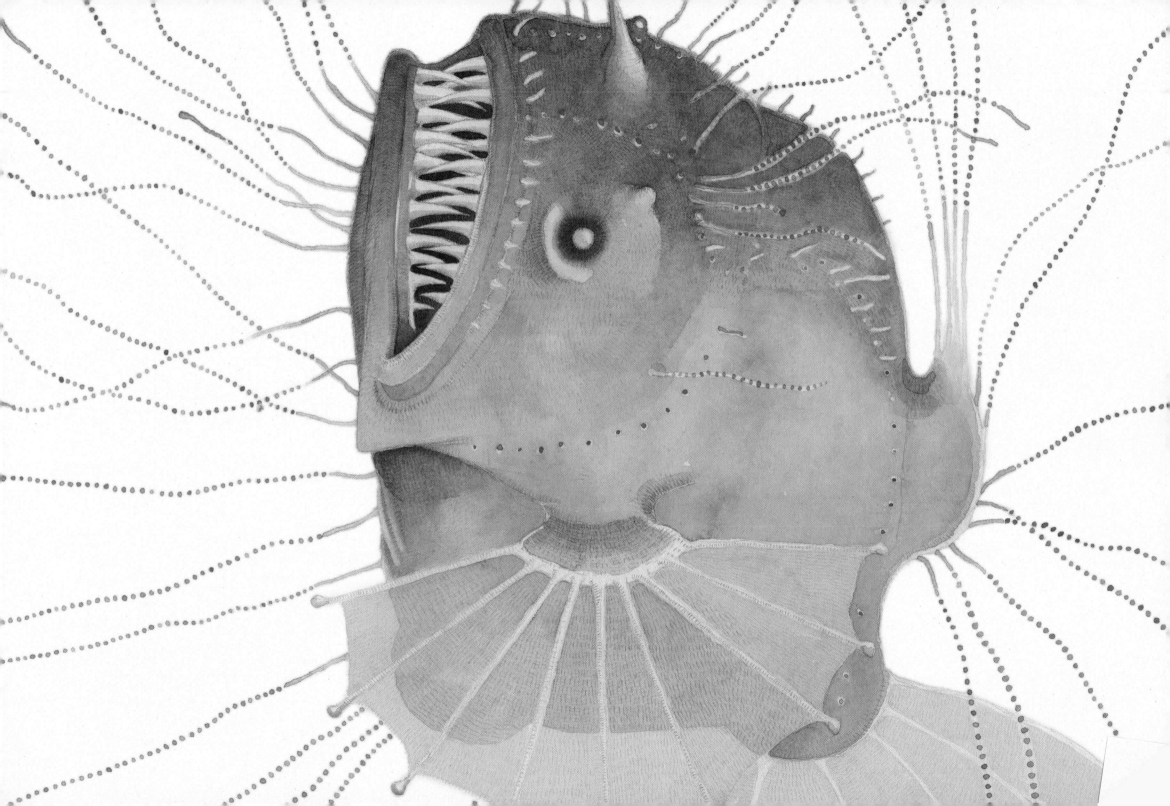

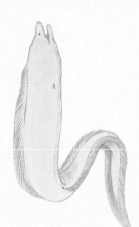

GREEN MORAY EEL

Despite their name, green moray eels are often brown. Their bodies are generally coated in a green-tinged mucus, which acts as a protective layer to keep their skin healthy. They use their elongated shapes to swim, flexing their bodies into curves to move through the water.

In Australia, green moray eels are particularly common along the lower east coast, from the bottom of Queensland right down to the middle of the Victorian coastline. They can also be found off the coast of parts of Tasmania, South Australia and Western Australia. They are fond of rocky reefs and areas with plenty of seaweed.

Green moray eels can swim backwards as well as forwards, which helps them to back neatly into hiding places in rocky areas. From there they can ambush prey, and hide from predators. Their jaws are lined with sharp teeth, and they also have an extra set of teeth tucked away on the roof of their mouths. These help them to hook in prey, which includes creatures such as fish, octopuses, squid, crabs and shrimp. Their sense of smell is very keen, and they rely on it when tracking down food.

Females release their eggs into the water, where they drift until they hatch into larval eels. Larval eels are small, flat and clear, and float in open waters until they develop and can move into more secluded habitats.

AUSTRALIAN FUR SEAL

Australian fur seals are found along the coast of Victoria and Tasmania, as well as parts of the New South Wales and South Australian coastlines. They spend a lot of time in rocky coastal areas or islands, where they come ashore to relax, moult and breed.

The males usually have coats in shades of dark brown and grey, with a thick, coarse section of hair around their necks. Females are often more of a silvery hue, and have cream-coloured chests and necks. Both males and females have long, sensitive whiskers sprouting from their faces, and their mouths are packed with sharp teeth.

Australian fur seals eat a lot of fish, plus squid, krill, octopuses, crustaceans and even some birds. They're magnificent swimmers – fast, agile and graceful. They can remain in the water for weeks at a time. The thick layer of fat under their skin helps keep them warm, and they have two layers of thick fur that keep their skin dry underwater.

On land, Australian fur seals can pull their bodies up and waddle along on all four flippers. They moult each year, coming to shore to shed their old fur and replace it with a fresh coat. They are highly social, and form colonies during breeding season. Large groups of females often live together on an island with one male, who fiercely defends his territory with roars, honks and growls. Females generally have only one pup, born in the summer months.

CORAL

Coral looks like a plant, but it is actually a number of very small creatures called polyps. Coral polyps can survive on their own, but they often band together to form a colony. Colonies then join up to create coral reefs. Coral reefs are vital to the health of the oceans – many different types of sea creatures rely on the habitat that coral reefs provide. Coral can survive for a very long time – polyps can live for hundreds of years, and colonies can thrive for several centuries. Some coral reefs started growing millions of years ago.

Coral is found in tropical waters, close enough to the surface that the sun can reach it. Australia has many incredible coral reefs, including the Great Barrier Reef off the coast of Queensland. It is the largest coral reef in the world, with hundreds of different species of coral.

Coral can be hard or soft. Hard coral polyps have six tentacles, while soft coral polyps have eight. The polyps on hard corals have a hard limestone skeleton that builds up layers over time and anchors them to things like rocks. The polyps on soft corals are supported by smaller limestone spikes.

Polyps don't naturally have any colour – they're translucent. The jewel-like colours of corals are caused by another living thing – a special kind of algae. The algae get nutrients from the sun, and then pass them on to the polyps. Things such as shifts in water temperature can cause coral to force out the algae living on them, causing coral to lose its colour. This is called coral bleaching and it can cause entire colonies to die.

The tentacles of coral polyps can sting and catch prey. They feed on passing creatures such as small fish and plankton, but they rely on the nutrients passed on by the algae they host to survive.

DUGONG

Dugongs are gentle, slow-moving creatures that are related to elephants.

They generally live in shallow coastal and inland areas, although sometimes they swim out into deeper waters. They can be found in the warmer waters around the top of Australia, from southern Queensland right around to northern Western Australia.

Dugongs are very large animals. They are grey or brown in colour, with bulbous bodies, long flippers and fluked tails. They have a broad, flat area around their mouths so that they can graze with ease along the ocean floor. Dugongs mostly forage for seagrasses, and their snuffling snouts leave trails in the seagrass and sand as they feed. Dugongs have sensitive bristles around their mouths that help them find food, but they are otherwise hairless. They also have tusks, but these are only visible on adult males and some older females.

Dugongs are usually solitary creatures, but they can live and feed in pairs, and sometimes large herds of them gather together. They have well-developed hearing and communicate with each other by making squeaking and pipping sounds.

In order to breathe, dugongs need to poke their nostrils out of the water. Sometimes they keep their tails on the seabed for balance as they raise their heads above water, so it looks as if they're standing. When they're first born, dugong babies need to be helped to the surface by their mothers so they can take their first breath.

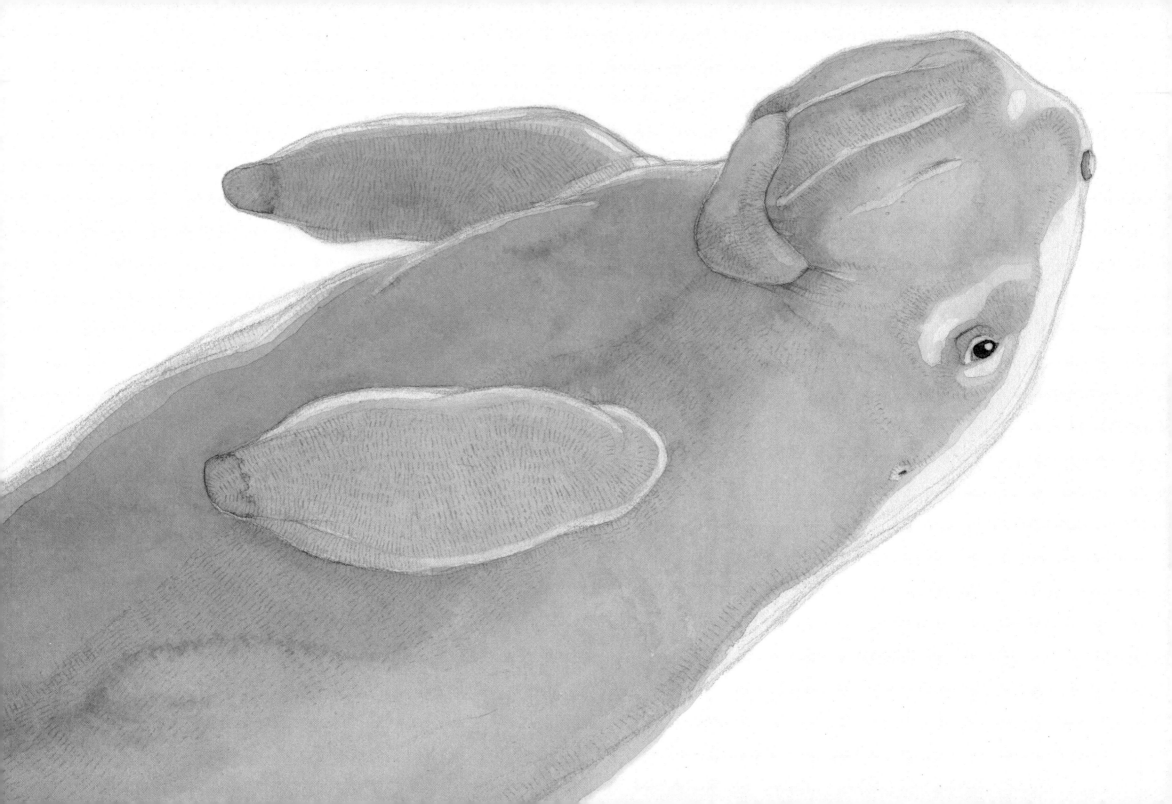

RED LIONFISH

Red lionfish, also called fire fish, zebra fish and scorpion-cod, live in warm, tropical waters. In Australia, they can be found along the top half of the coastline, along the west coast right around to New South Wales. They live in coral reefs and rocky areas, often hiding out near caves, ledges and crevices.

Red lionfish are covered with bold red-and-cream stripes, with long fins sprouting from the tops of their bodies and extending out on either side. They have a number of sharp, highly venomous spines on top of their bodies, but they don't use them to hunt – the venom is purely for self-defence.

Their diet generally includes such things as fish, shrimp and small crabs. They often ambush their prey by staying still, or moving very slowly, then lunging suddenly to catch unsuspecting animals. They also hunt actively, sometimes fanning out their long fins to direct fish into a place where it is easier to catch them.

Female red lionfish release huge numbers of eggs into the water, where they are fertilised by males and then left to float along until they hatch.

BOTTLENOSE DOLPHIN

Bottlenose dolphins are generally grey, with a curved dorsal fin and a white underbelly. Their rounded snout is slightly curved, and it often looks as if they are grinning.

They can be found all around the coast of Australia – some make their homes in sheltered bays, while others live further out to sea. Bottlenose dolphins are excellent divers and strong swimmers. They come to the surface of the water regularly to breathe through their blowholes, and sometimes leap out of the water in graceful arcs.

Bottlenose dolphins are social and very talkative, making such sounds as whistles, grunts, squeaks, clicks and trills. When hunting for food, they use echolocation. They make up to one thousand clicking sounds per second, which travel through the ocean and send back echoes to let the dolphins know what's nearby.

A bottlenose dolphin's diet is very broad, and includes fish, squid and crustaceans. They usually swallow their prey whole, and sometimes work together to round up groups of fish so they're easier to catch.

A group of dolphins is called a pod. Each dolphin helps take care of any babies born into the pod. Bottlenose dolphins are known for being remarkably compassionate. If one of their pod is injured, they will help them up to the water's surface so they can breathe. They can even come to the rescue of other animals.

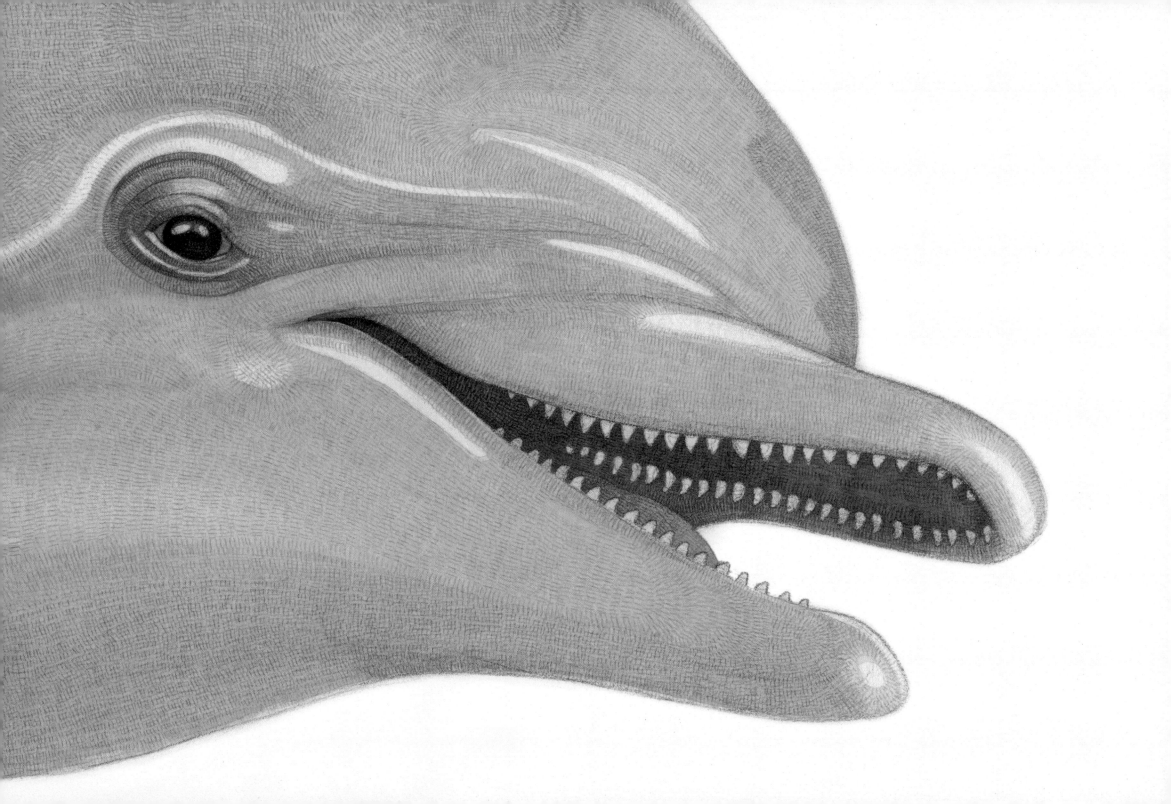

SOLDIER CRAB

Soldier crabs have small, rounded bodies with a distinctive blue tint. Their legs are long, thin and cream-coloured, with bars of deep purple at each joint.

They like sandy environments, and often make their homes in intertidal flats, estuaries and mangroves. Soldier crabs are particularly common along the east coast of Australia, but can also be found along the top of the country and down into the middle of the Western Australian coastline.

Soldier crabs hunt together in huge troops, clearing out every speck of food from the beach one section at a time. They eat by shoving sand into their mouths with their claws, sifting through it inside their mouths for things like algae and snail eggs, then spitting out the leftover sand in pellets.

Unlike many other crabs, soldier crabs walk forwards instead of sideways. They forage at low tide, emerging from their sandy burrows to march across the beach. The smooth sand becomes covered in tiny bumps as hundreds of tiny crabs dig for food. Then, before the tide comes back up and washes them away, they twist themselves back down into their sandy burrows.

STINGRAY

Many different species of stingray can be found in Australian waters. They generally live in tropical and temperate areas, and favour shallow waters with sandy or muddy bottoms.

Stingrays have flattened bodies, with two very large fins stretching out on either side like wings. Some species flap these fins to swim through the water, but others undulate their bodies to swim in a graceful, sweeping motion. Stingrays are not constantly active and spend a lot of time partially buried under the sand, usually with part of their tail protruding. Some species have tails with sharp, serrated spines or barbs laced with a powerful venom that can be used for self-defence.

Stingrays can be solitary animals, but some species migrate or feed in large groups. They hunt such prey as crustaceans, fish, shrimp, snails and worms using electrical sensors, which are little hollows around their mouths filled with a jelly-like substance. These sensors help them find prey by picking up the small electrical charges of other animals as they move in the water.

Stingray skin can be smooth or have a rough, granular texture. Stingrays are usually brown or grey on top with a pale belly underneath, and some have black, white, or even bright blue speckles. Their mouths, nostrils and gills are all hidden away on their underbelly, and their eyes are on the sides of their bodies.

Female stingrays hold their eggs inside their bodies to incubate them, then give birth to live babies.

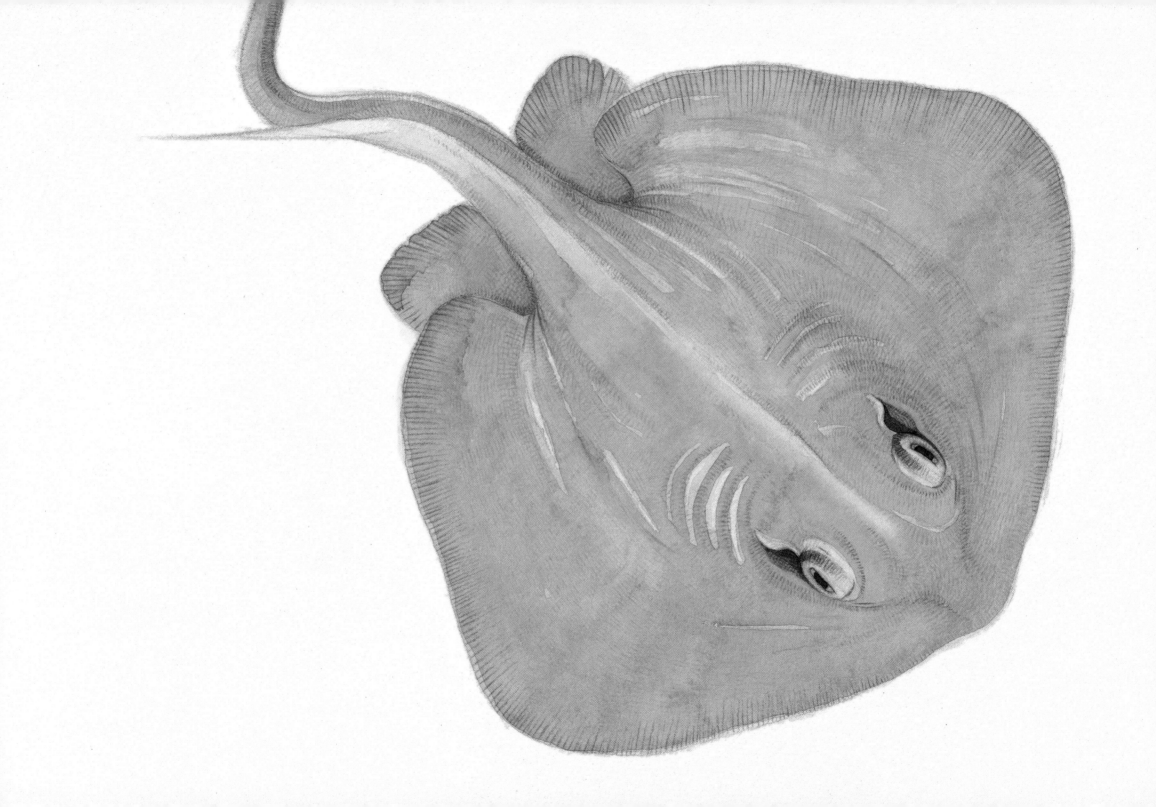

NUDIBRANCH

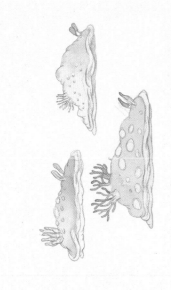

Nudibranchs are a type of sea slug, and there are hundreds of different species living in Australian waters. They are particularly common around reefs, but can be found in a broad range of environments. Nudibranch bodies come in many different sizes, and many species have shapes protruding from their bodies, including raised bumps, feathery tails, frills, spikes and horns.

Most nudibranchs are brightly coloured and beautifully patterned, with spots, stripes, swirls, speckles and rings of colour. These colours protect them from predators, either by helping them blend into their environments, or by acting as a warning. Many nudibranchs absorb toxins from their food, which in turn make them toxic to predators. These nudibranchs often have bright skin to let predators know to leave them alone.

Nudibranchs eat things like coral, algae, sea sponges, anemones and barnacles. They locate food using two very sensitive tentacles on their head called 'rhinophores'. They have poor eyesight, so they rely on smell, taste and touch to sense the world around them.

Each nudibranch is both male and female. They can lay huge numbers of eggs, which often form ribbon-like coils that can be quite beautiful. When they hatch, young nudibranchs go through a larval stage before maturing fully.

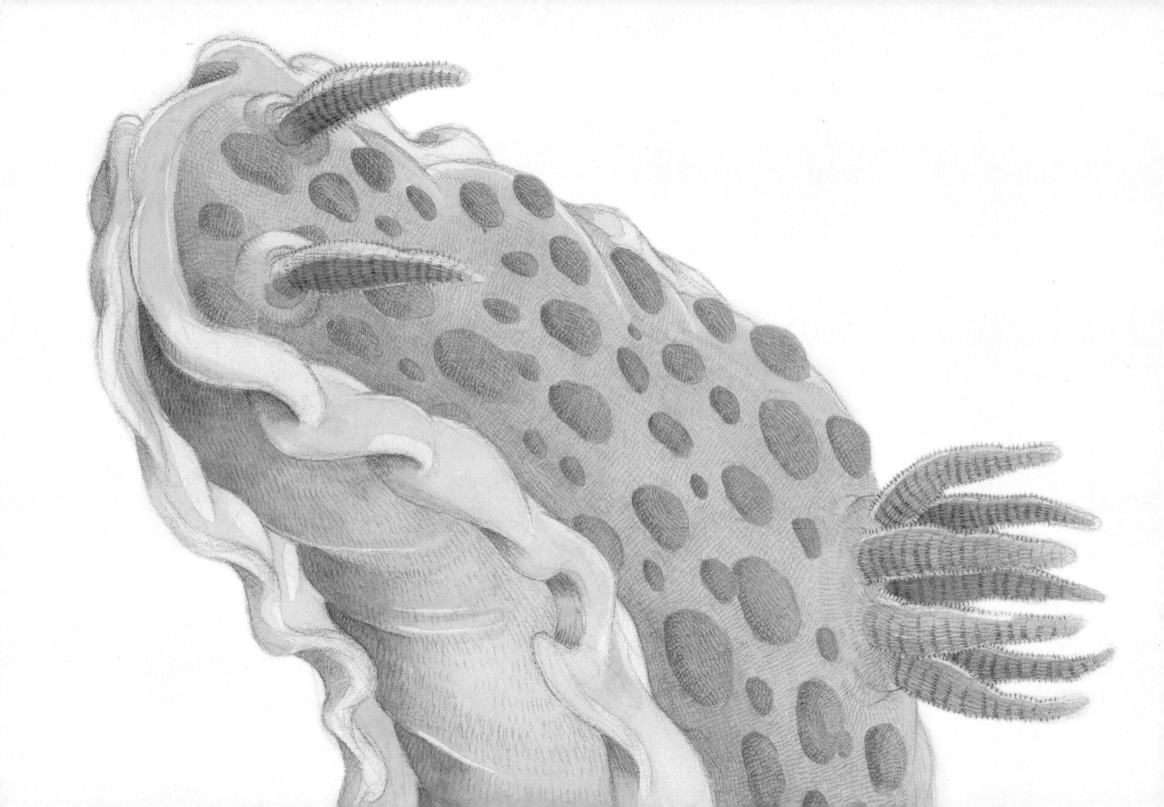

BLUEBOTTLE

A bluebottle is made up of four different creatures called 'zooids'. No single zooid can survive alone, but together they work like one unified animal.

One zooid is the float, which glides on top of the water like a translucent bubble. It is filled with gas and can contract and expand like a balloon. Each float has vivid blue highlights, and sometimes hints of purple, pink or pale green, too. Floats are topped with frilled crests, which catch the wind and steer bluebottles in different directions.

Another zooid is the tentacles that trail through the water below the float, and latch onto food. Bluebottles eat small sea creatures, including fish, crustaceans and molluscs. They use one particularly long tentacle to hunt, which has tiny, toxic barbs on it to stop prey from escaping. Bluebottle tentacles can still sting even if they have washed up on the shore.

The third zooid acts as the mouth and stomach, eating anything the tentacles catch, and the fourth zooid is for reproduction. Bluebottle eggs hatch into larvae, which become individual zooids. These zooids then come together with others to form new bluebottles.

Bluebottles generally prefer slightly warmer waters. They can typically be found along the east coast of Australia in summer and the lower half of the Western Australian coast in the cooler months.

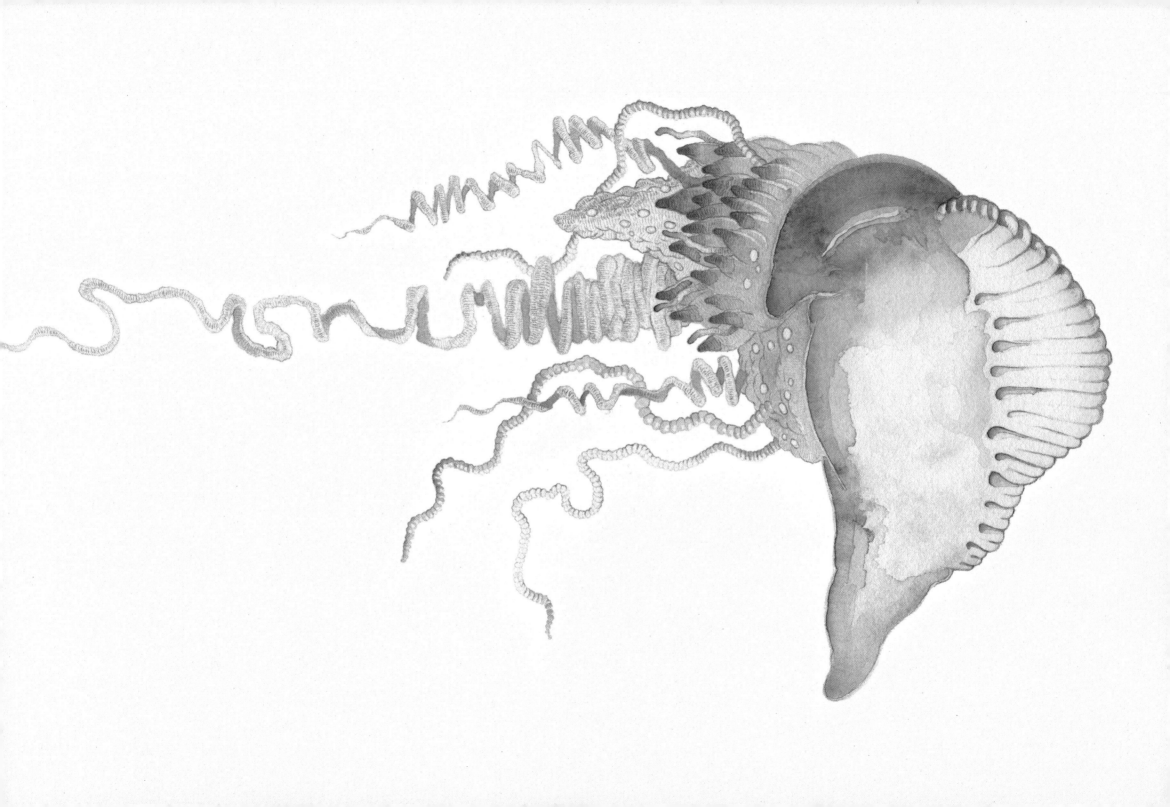

WEEDY SEA DRAGON

Weedy sea dragons have long, slender bodies with copious amounts of leafy shapes sprouting from them. Colours and patterns vary, but their skin often has red and yellow tones, with blue stripes and white or yellow spots.

Weedy sea dragons are endemic to Australian waters – they are not found anywhere else in the world. They live around the top half of the Australian coastline, from New South Wales to Western Australia. They prefer to live on reefs, or in kelp forests and seagrass beds, where they can camouflage themselves.

Weedy sea dragons are not particularly good swimmers. Their tails can't grip onto plants to anchor themselves like seahorses do, so they're largely at the mercy of the currents – they sway and drift just like fronds of seaweed.

When they're courting, pairs of weedy sea dragons dance together each day for weeks. Males carry distinctive pink eggs in a spongy area beneath their tails. At any one time, there can be hundreds of eggs tucked under there. Each weedy sea dragon baby is tiny, but fully formed when it hatches.

Weedy sea dragons eat with their long, thin snouts, sucking up things like plankton, fish larvae, small crustaceans and tiny worms. They need to eat almost constantly to keep their energy up.

BLUE-RINGED OCTOPUS

Blue-ringed octopuses are small, extremely dangerous creatures that live in coastal waters around Australia. They make their homes in places with plenty of crevices and shells to hide amongst, including rock pools, coral reefs and rocky beaches.

There are a number of blue-ringed octopus species. Their skin is patterned in shades of brown and cream – it's only when they're scared that they flash with electric blue rings. These bright, pulsing colours are a warning to predators. If that warning doesn't work, blue-ringed octopuses can use their powerful venom to defend themselves. The stinging part of a blue-ringed octopus's body is very small, but their venom is lethal. Despite this, blue-ringed octopuses are not aggressive – they're shy and reclusive, and prefer to hide rather than attack.

Blue-ringed octopuses eat things like crabs, shrimp and small fish, using their venom to paralyse prey before eating it.

The females carry their eggs securely tucked away underneath their eight tentacles. They take excellent care of them, keeping constant guard until they hatch. Mothers do not generally live for long once their eggs have hatched.

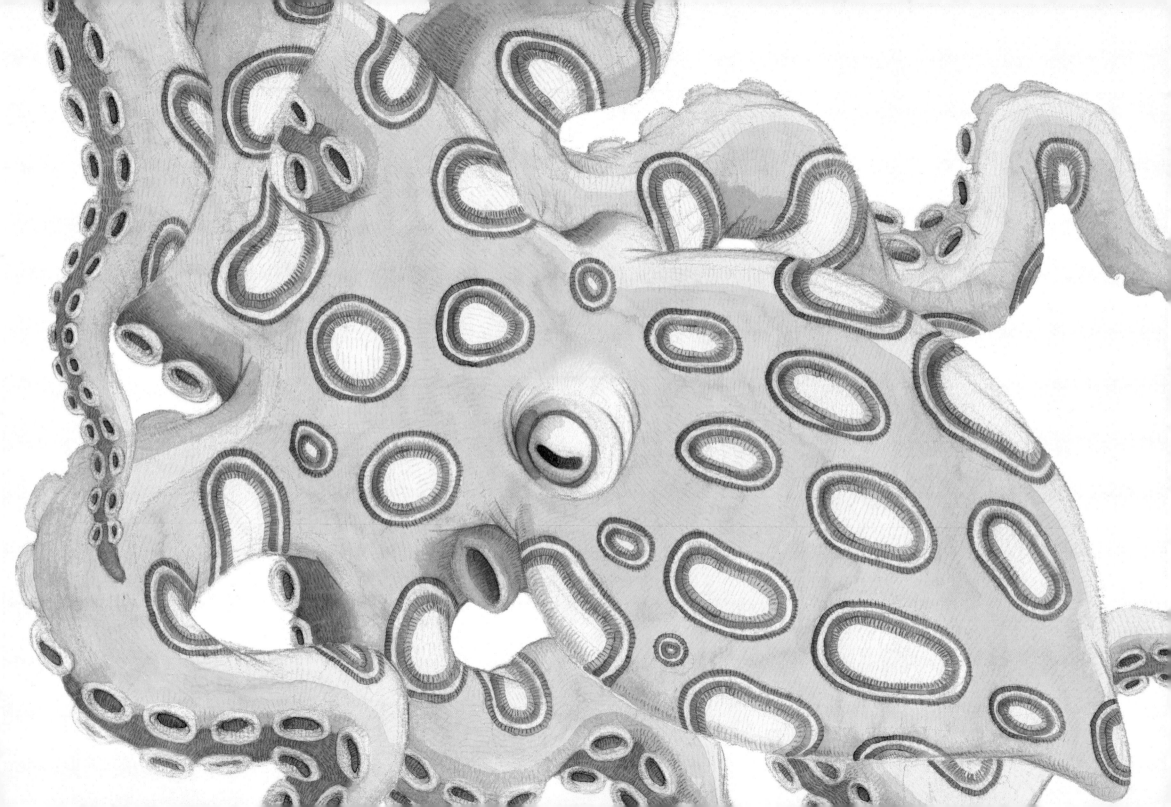

GREEN SEA TURTLE

Green sea turtles have large, teardrop-shaped shells in shades of brown, green and yellow, and their skin has a distinctive greenish hue. They live in warm waters, often near coral reefs or seagrass beds. These turtles are particularly common in the Great Barrier Reef – one of the largest nesting populations in the world can be found there. They also live right along the coast of Queensland, over the top of the country and down into the middle of the Western Australian coastline.

Green sea turtles spend most of their time in the water, using their broad flippers to glide long distances through the ocean. They can stay underwater for hours at a time, but generally surface to breathe quite regularly. They often swim near the surface of the ocean where the sun's rays soak through, and they occasionally crawl onto land to sunbathe.

Green sea turtles lay their eggs on land, and they like to return to the beach where they were born to do it. Even if it is thousands of kilometres away, and they haven't been there for years, they still know the way back. Females dig a deep pit on the beach with their flippers, lay their eggs inside and cover them with sand before swimming back into the ocean. About two months later, the tiny hatchlings dig their way out and head for the water.

Green sea turtles are herbivores, foraging for things like seaweed, algae and seagrass. When they're young, their diet also includes such things as plankton, jellies and crabs.

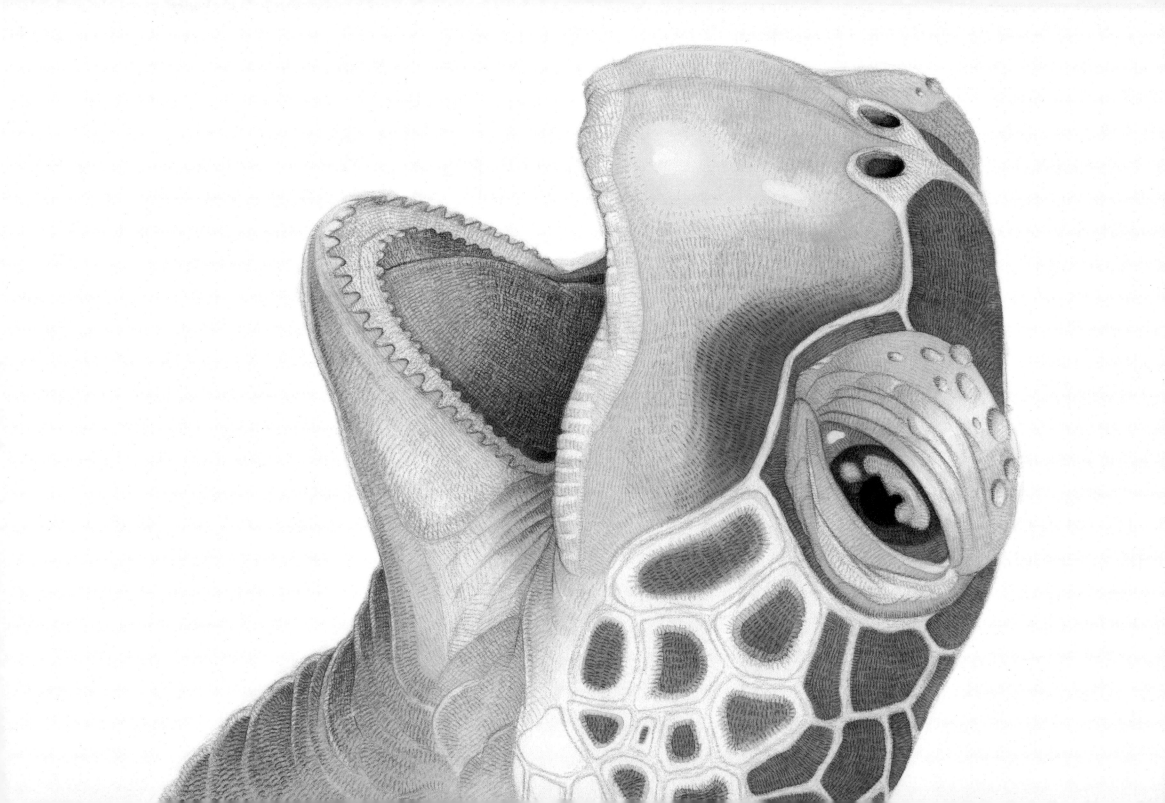

Little Hare Books
an imprint of
Hardie Grant Egmont
Ground Floor, Building 1, 658 Church Street
Richmond, Victoria 3121, Australia

www.littleharebooks.com

First published 2019

A catalogue record for this
book is available from the
National Library of Australia

NATIONAL
LIBRARY
OF AUSTRALIA

9781760504694 (hbk.)

Designed by Pooja Desai
Text by Ella Meave
Produced by Pica Digital, Singapore
Printed through Asia Pacific Offset
Printed in Shenzhen, Guangdong Province, China

5 4 3 2 1